E♭ ALTO CLARINET

CONCERT FAVORITES

Volume 1

Band Arrangements Correlated with
Essential Elements Band Method Book 1

Page	Title	Composer/Arranger	Correlated with Essential Elements
2	Let's Rock	Michael Sweeney	Book 1, page 11
3	Majestic March	Paul Lavender	Book 1, page 11
4	Mickey Mouse March	arr. Michael Sweeney	Book 1, page 11
5	Power Rock	arr. Michael Sweeney	Book 1, page 11
6	When The Saints Go Marching In	arr. John Higgins	Book 1, page 11
7	Farandole	arr. Michael Sweeney	Book 1, page 24
8	Jus' Plain Blues	Michael Sweeney	Book 1, page 24
9	My Heart Will Go On	arr. Paul Lavender	Book 1, page 24
10	Rainbow Connection	arr. Paul Lavender	Book 1, page 24
11	Supercalifragilisticexpialidocious	arr. Michael Sweeney	Book 1, page 24
12	Do-Re-Mi	arr. Paul Lavender	Book 1, page 34
13	Drums Of Corona	Michael Sweeney	Book 1, page 34
14	Laredo (Concert March)	John Higgins	Book 1, page 34
15	Pomp And Circumstance	arr. Michael Sweeney	Book 1, page 34
16	Stratford March	John Higgins	Book 1, page 34

ISBN 978-0-634-05203-9

HAL•LEONARD®
7777 W. BLUEMOUND RD. P.O. BOX 13819 MILWAUKEE, WI 53213

00860123

LET'S ROCK!

Eb ALTO CLARINET

MICHAEL SWEENEY (ASCAP)

00860123

E♭ ALTO CLARINET

By PAUL LAVENDER

00860123

MICKEY MOUSE MARCH
(From Walt Disney's "THE MICKEY MOUSE CLUB")

Eb ALTO CLARINET

Words and Music by JIMMIE DODD
Arranged by MICHAEL SWEENEY

March Tempo

00860123

POWER ROCK
(We Will Rock You • Another One Bites The Dust)

Eb ALTO CLARINET

Arranged by MICHAEL SWEENEY

00860123

WHEN THE SAINTS GO MARCHING IN

Words by KATHERINE E. PURVIS
Music by JAMES M. BLACK
Arranged by JOHN HIGGINS

Eb ALTO CLARINET

March Style

FARANDOLE
(From "L'Arlésienne")

Eb ALTO CLARINET

GEORGES BIZET
Arranged by MICHAEL SWEENEY (ASCAP)

00860123

8

JU' PLAIN BLUES

Eb ALTO CLARINET

MICHAEL SWEENEY (ASCAP)

From the Paramount and Twentieth Century Fox Motion Picture TITANIC

MY HEART WILL GO ON

(Love Theme From 'Titanic')

Music by JAMES HORNER
Lyric by WILL JENNINGS
Arranged by PAUL LAVENDER

Eb ALTO CLARINET

Moderately

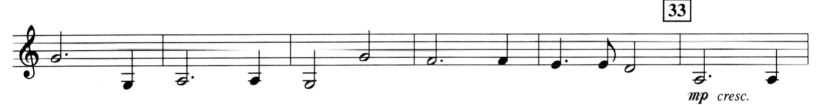

From THE MUPPET MOVIE

THE rAINBOW CᴜNNECTION

Words and Music by PAUL WILLIAMS
and KENNITH L. ASCHER
Arranged by PAUL LAVENDER

E♭ ALTO CLARINET

00860123

From Walt Disney's MARY POPPINS

SUPER-CALIF-RAGILISTI-EX-PIALI-DO-TIOUS

Words and Music by
RICHARD M. SHERMAN and **ROBERT B. SHERMAN**
Arranged by MICHAEL SWEENEY

E♭ ALTO CLARINET

Moderately

00860123

(From "THE SOUND OF MUSIC")
DO-RE-MI

Eb **Alto Clarinet**

Lyrics by OSCAR HAMMERSTEIN II
Music by RICHARD RODGERS
Arranged by PAUL LAVENDER

E♭ ALTO CLARINET

MICHAEL SWEENEY (ASCAP)

00860123

LAREDO
(Concert March)

E♭ ALTO CLARINET

JOHN HIGGINS

00860123

POMP AND CIRCUMSTANCE
March No. 1

Eb ALTO CLARINET

By EDWARD ELGAR
Arranged by MICHAEL SWEENEY

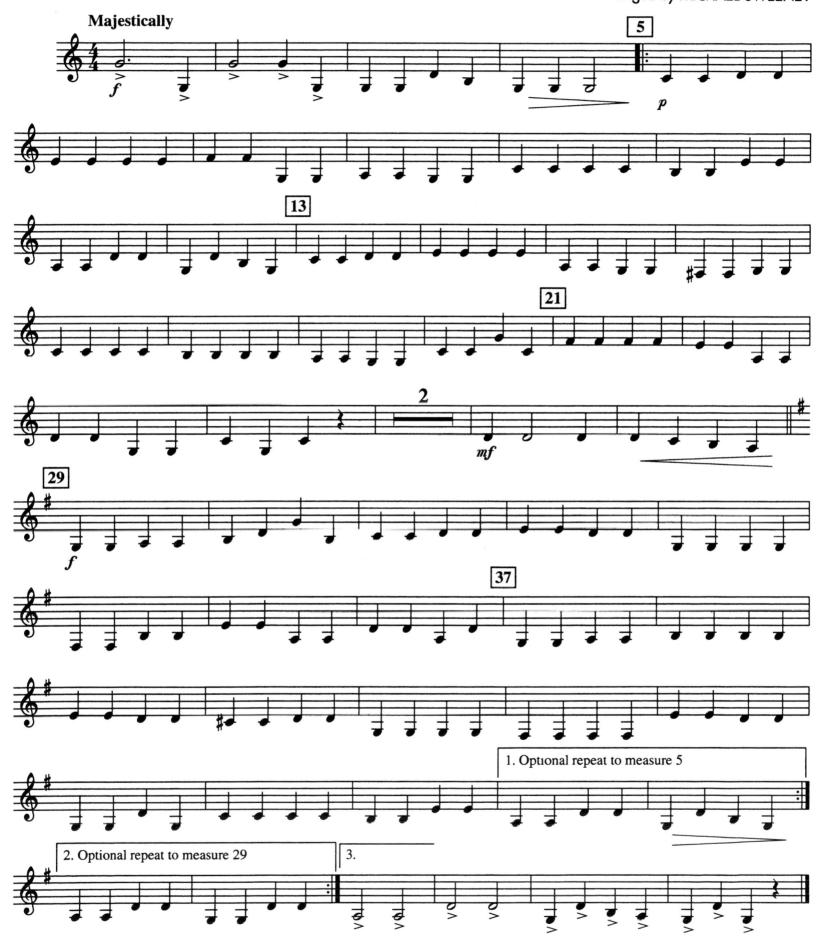

00860123

STRATFORD MARCH

Eb ALTO CLARINET

JOHN HIGGINS (ASCAP)